Special
Our Hero

James Tyrone "J.T." Martin, Sr.

To the readers of this amazing story, "thank you" for investing your time and resources into exploring my father-in-law's life journey. You will cry, laugh, and cheer as you navigate through his remarkable story of courage, determination, and perseverance. As you reflect on how he not only survived, but thrived in the world he inhabited–I hope you will eagerly share his extraordinary story with family, friends, and neighbors. Read on as you enter, "Vaulting Over Destiny."

Ava Martin
June 27, 2017

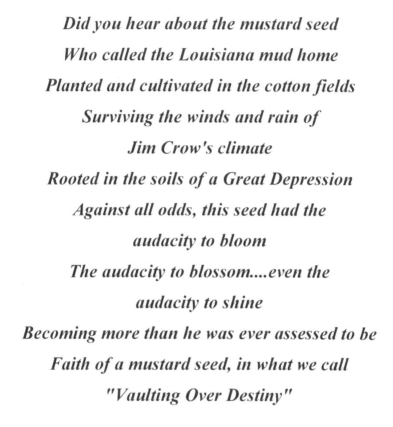

Did you hear about the mustard seed

Who called the Louisiana mud home

Planted and cultivated in the cotton fields

Surviving the winds and rain of

Jim Crow's climate

Rooted in the soils of a Great Depression

Against all odds, this seed had the

audacity to bloom

The audacity to blossom....even the

audacity to shine

Becoming more than he was ever assessed to be

Faith of a mustard seed, in what we call

"Vaulting Over Destiny"

Nick Martin
(Grandson)
June 29, 2017

"Vaulting Over Destiny" is a true tale of what it means to be brave, hardworking and overall confident about life. My grandfather, J.T. Martin, Sr. rose above unbelievable expectations in order to provide for his family and himself. He didn't let anything, not even an injury prevented him from achieving his accomplishments. I believe those who read his story will be fully engaged and enthralled by everything that this dynamic individual has to offer. His story reminds us that "nothing is impossible as long as you're willing to persevere." I see "Vaulting Over Destiny" as an unforgettable work of art and a classic for years to come.

Rachel Martin
June 26, 2017

VAULTING OVER DESTINY

A Story of Favor, Faith & Determination

By
Col. (Ret.)
Jeremy M. Martin

To Stefani --
Thanks for your great support!
A great pleasure to meet and
speak with you!
All The Best,
Col Jy Martin

CONTENTS

FOREWORD

"Vaulting Over Destiny" is a real life American success story about a child born to sharecroppers in the Deep South, on the eve of the Great Depression. A compelling story of a boy named James Thomas Martin, Sr. who despite incredible odds against him, cheated death and refused to allow the hand of life dealt to him to determine his destiny. James Thomas Martin, Sr. or "J.T.," the main source for this story's central character, is my dad.

J.T. has lived a full, rich life, as he approaches 89 years of age. Another key source who provided critically sensitive information concerning his early years was his mom, the late Lucy Hunter Hawkins. There are also stories from relatives and friends including his younger sister, Mable Martin Hales. These stories have been celebrated and repeated over the years at family reunions and other family gatherings for generations.

J.T. was born in southern Alabama. Before the age of one, he moved with his parents to northeast Louisiana, where his dad found work as a sharecropper. He would face incredible odds growing up in the Deep South; from struggling to receive a quality education in separate but unequal schools, to poor health care. An even larger challenge loomed in trying to rise above the meager standard of living established by his parents and grandparents, who both toiled amid the withering oppression of Jim Crow, a post reconstruction system of institutionalized social oppression, which limited the freedom of black Americans.

J.T. would endure a horrific tragedy before his second birthday. After miraculously surviving the devastating accident, he would vigorously respond and display the inner strength and resiliency that would alter and define his character for life.

His life is a story of perseverance and strength. Though severely wounded and traumatized by a tragic accident, which resulted in the loss of his left leg, he responded in a manner which amazed his family and an entire community. Determined to be accepted by his family and friends, and not be viewed as an invalid, he drove himself to achieve physical exploits which far exceeded many who suffered a similar handicap.

In addition to overcoming the physical challenges of such a daunting handicap, he had to endure the mental challenges as well. Every time he walked into a room, people would be visibly moved. Children would point and ask their parents or him, "What happened to your leg?" About the time he settled into a rhythm in his life, his world would take another traumatic turn.

J.T. loved his dad and he was motivated to overcome his handicap by a deep desire to please him. When he was in his early teen years, his dad abandoned the family, which included him and three younger siblings. Now he was the "man of the house."

In addition to attending school, he took on part-time work to help lighten the burden on his mom, who worked as a domestic, cleaning houses and hand-washing clothes to sustain her family.

Despite not being encouraged to seek higher education, he always had a burning desire to go to college. He had overcome overwhelming obstacles in his life, and becoming the first male in his family to finish high school and attend college would be another. You'll be inspired by his commitment to achieve his goals, which ultimately changed the trajectory of his life.

In the pages that follow, you'll be treated to a great American story of perseverance, strength, and courage. A true triumph of the human spirit!

Chapter One

Birth In LA
(Lower Alabama)

The life journey for J.T. began in the early fall of 1928, in the piney woods of southern Alabama, near the town of Camden. J.T., short for James Thomas, was born into the home of Willis Martin, Sr. and Lucy Hunter.

J.T.'s dad was a farmer, and so was his paternal grandfather. Willis Martin, Sr. as well as his parents, brothers and sisters, and the entire Martin family in the Camden area, were slave descendants and survivors of the failed post-Civil War Reconstruction era. The absence of a government backed credit system, and no job training skills, relegated many blacks to work on farms owned by former Confederate slave owners and their descendants. Uneducated and with virtually no political or economic power, the Martins, like many southern families during this time frame were left to scratch out a living on the farm, in the only life they'd ever known.

Willis Martin, Sr. was a hard worker. He was considered by many to be an excellent farmer and for a time a good provider for his family. However, stories from family and friends alike reveal that his farming prowess did not always carry over into his most important role, that of husband and dad. Owing to a mountain of revelations and legendary stories about Willis's exploits, one glaringly revealed later in this book, a general statement concluding that Willis worked very hard, and that he played extremely hard, seems more than generous. J.T.'s mom, Lucy, was gentle and subservient. Tall, lean, with Native American features, she worked hard to take care of her children. She toiled on the farm in the cotton and sweet potato fields, alongside her husband, or sometimes inside cleaning and cooking in the home of the landowner. A brief conversation with Lucy would have quickly revealed her lack of formal education. But those who know her story simply marvel at her remarkable inner strength and unbreakable will. It was into this challenging environment that little J.T. was born on September 19, 1928, the third of seven children. Around the time of J.T.'s birth a couple of his dad's brothers had departed Alabama and moved to Northeast Louisiana. They encouraged Willis to move his family as well.

The Martins were farmers, and cotton was still king in the south. Willis' brothers were convinced that the land in Louisiana was more conducive to growing cotton. They believed better tenant opportunities existed for sharecroppers, and that the cotton yield would lead to more wages and a better quality of life.

In 1929, the year the Great Depression began, Willis Martin would move his family, including little J.T., to Northeast

Louisiana, in search of a better life. They settled near Oak Grove, Louisiana, a segregated town of roughly 1,200 residents.

Chapter Two

EXODUS

Leaving their home and way of life in Alabama must have been quite an adjustment for Willis Martin and his family. Arriving in Louisiana, it was now time to get settled into a new environment and a new way of life. Willis had arrived in the land of cotton, and now he would apply his farming skills in the fertile farmland of Northeast Louisiana.

The family settled into their new environment as sharecroppers. They signed a contract with a white landowner which allowed them to live in a tenant home on the landowner's property. Willis and his family could use the land in return for a share of the crops produced on their portion of the land. The home they were assigned was a "shotgun house" with an added bedroom.

A shotgun house is a rectangular shaped house no more than 12-13 feet wide with rooms one behind the other and doors at each end of the house. The house needed work, but it offered adequate shelter until repairs could be made. There was no indoor plumbing, so a wooden outhouse had to be constructed away from the main house. There was no plumbing in the outhouse. It was a pit variety, and heavy lime was used to manage the odor.

In the waning weeks of the summer of 1930, as little J.T. approached his second birthday, the family's transition to Louisiana was nearly complete. The Martin family had been received favorably by their landowners. First-hand accounts from J.T.'s mom, Lucy, affirm that the landowner was a decent man who had treated her family well during the transition. Things were looking up for the family in their new environment.

Chapter Three

CHEATING
DEATH

Little J.T. was growing like a weed during that summer of 1930, and getting into everything! He was a precocious child, and the apple of his dad's eye. J.T. gazed with wonder as he saw his daddy and family members return home from the farm and cotton fields after a hard day of work. Day after day, he longed to join his dad at work, but alas, he was too young, and he spent his days playing around the house. The family dog, Shep, was his chief playmate.

On one fateful July day, when J.T. was 22 months old, he watched his dad leave home and take a short walk to a sawmill (lumber mill) not far from the landowner's property. The sawmill was a place where trees and logs were cut by powerful circular saws with very sharp blades. He waited a bit, and then unnoticed, he left the house, accompanied by Shep, to follow his dad. J.T. and Shep arrived at the sawmill undetected.

J.T. anxiously gazed around the mill. He was in unfamiliar territory. As a small, innocent child, he was incapable of sensing the hazardous environment he had entered. Unable to spot his dad, the little tyke continued his curious travel as he sauntered around the mill, with Shep close behind.

Finally, little J.T. heard grown up voices. His dad must be near. My daddy will be glad to see me, he must have thought. He'll pick me up in his arms the way, he does when he comes home in the evenings. To better gauge where the voices were coming from J.T. decided to climb up on this apparatus to get a better look. Little did he know it was an active bandsaw. It cut into J.T.'s left leg below the knee. He was frightened, and he knew he was badly hurt. But somehow, he couldn't scream, maybe he was in shock! Thankfully, Shep had followed him out of the house. The faithful dog knew J.T. was in trouble and hurt badly. According to the eye witness account of the man who initially found J.T. that fateful morning, Shep barked as fiercely and loudly as ever. His bark alerted the men working at the sawmill, including his dad, that something was terribly wrong.

Willis Martin was crushed when he saw his little son. Little J.T.'s left leg was dangling below the knee. He'd lost a lot of blood and was still bleeding profusely. There was panic and anxiety among the men. They needed to stop the bleeding. Could the leg be re-attached? Was the little child going to die? None of the black men working at the mill owned a car. Someone screamed to get the vehicle so they could rush little J.T. into town to the doctor's office. Perhaps the doctor could save his life, if not his little leg.

Suddenly, J.T.'s mom, Lucy, appeared. While out in the front yard looking for J.T., she was somehow drawn to the mill by the frantic noise and commotion emanating from the men. She screamed, and almost collapsed, when she saw her severely injured baby boy. In her anguish, she cried out to heaven for help. "Oh, God, don't let my baby die!"

J.T. was rushed to the doctor's office. Thankfully the doctor was in and he proceeded to immediately take care of J.T. Very soon after his examination he confirmed J.T.'s parents worst fears, that the leg could not be saved. The only question that remained in the doctor's mind was where to make the amputation. The saw at the mill had torn into J.T.'s leg below the knee. Having lost a significant amount of blood, there was a serious threat of infection. The doctor believed that making the amputation half way above the knee would give J.T. the best chance of survival.

The little boy would now have to essentially go through a second amputation on the very same day. The second amputation would be preceded by pain killers, but that was no less traumatic for J.T.'s parents, who were in shock as they pondered the immediate and future fate of their baby boy. He'd just begun to hit his stride walking and beginning to run; would he ever walk again? Will he be an invalid all his life…? Would he survive the amputation? Oh, God, dear Jesus, help us. In what can only be described as a miracle; little J.T. survived the surgery. The doctor literally marveled at the little boy's resiliency and strong will. The immediate days ahead would be tough for J.T., and his entire family.

There would be medication and painkillers, doctor's visits, and many sleepless nights. A summer day which began like most days on the farm, had ended in tragedy, with the near loss of a promising child's life. The days and weeks ahead would be challenging, and test the spirit and resiliency of the entire family.

Chapter Four

THE LONG ROAD TO RECOVERY

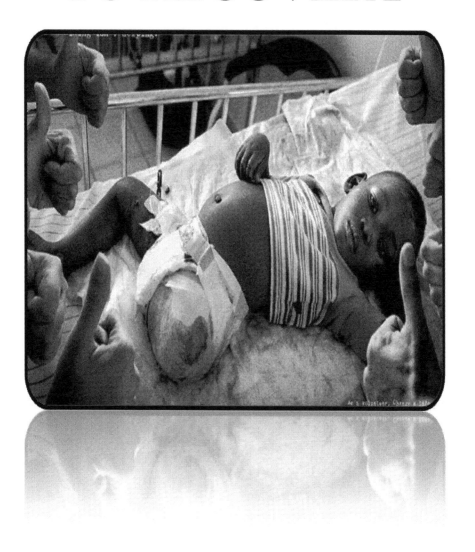

Little J.T.'s tragic injury, and near death experience severely traumatized his entire family. Divine intervention had saved his life, but what kind of life would he experience? His parents were distraught. Protecting children is an instinctive quality ingrained into parents. J.T.'s parents continued to revisit their actions on that fateful morning. How could we have let this happen? Who was responsible for watching him? If only I'd been more attentive. Neither of them even considered he'd attempt to leave the yard for the mill. It's a question that J.T.'s mom would frequently ponder in her heart for the rest of her life.

For the first few weeks J.T. was under constant medical care from the town doctor. The doctor marveled at J.T.'s resilience and will to live. He grew very fond of the little boy.

After several weeks, it became apparent that J.T. would survive the horrific accident. But he would now have to come to terms with his new predicament. He likely had plenty of questions for his mom and dad. One can imagine his mom bathing him and keeping the wound clean and dressed.

Perhaps little J.T. would question her at times during the process. "Mama, is my leg going to grow back? Will I be able to walk and run again, and chase Shep around the house, Mama?"

And how might his mom have responded to such an innocent question from her child?

In an almost inconceivable twist of fate, the family's long nightmare was interrupted by J.T.'s incredible response to treatment and strong positive attitude. He was a true wonder kid. He was an inspiration to not just those in the black community, but to the entire village. The folks in that deeply religious community knew that God almighty had answered their prayers and saved a child from certain death.

With the portion of J.T.'s severed limb now completely healed, it was time to start the rehabilitation process.

Aside from the agonizing loss of a limb, J.T. was healthy. He was a talented little boy now nearly three years old. He was aggressive, athletic, and physically capable to make the transition to crutches to increase his mobility. The rehabilitation process was slow and methodical. J.T. had to adjust to two crutches, strengthen his upper body to support his weight, and maintain the balance of maneuvering his single leg and body as a cohesive unit. He fell frequently in those early days of rehabilitation, but he kept at it. Just as he seemed to be making real progress with the crutches, his dad threw him a real curve!

As he did most days, J.T.'s dad came home from work one evening around supper time. Little J.T. was practicing with his crutches, no doubt seeking his Dad's approval or encouragement for his progress.

Willis closely observed his son's efforts, locked in an intense gaze as J.T. moved slowly with the two crutches. Suddenly Willis jumped from his chair, startling everyone in the room. "Son you don't need no two crutches, you just need one. Lucy, if he learns to walk with that one crutch it'll be like another leg…I'm telling you, he don't need no two crutches." J.T.'s dad took away the crutch from under his right arm. He believed that if J.T. would use the crutch under his left arm it would make him more maneuverable, and keep his right arm free.

After considerable time spent using two crutches, it was not an easy transition for J.T. to use one crutch. He fell time after time as he tried to shift his weight and adjust to one crutch. He desperately wanted to maintain two crutches. He'd mastered the process, felt comfortable, and felt a sense of accomplishment that he'd achieved adequate mobility. But his dad wouldn't relent; he hid the second crutch and was determined to coach J.T. to use the single crutch. J.T. slowly began to master the process of using the single crutch. Like every challenge the young child had faced to date, he responded positively, never crying and never quitting.

Many years later, J.T. would comment that his dad insisting that he used one crutch was perhaps, the greatest single gift he would ever give him, other than life itself.

Chapter Five

BABY SISTER & INNOVATIVE HOME SCHOOL

After being watched over and coddled for a long period following the accident, it slowly became clear to J.T.'s parents, and his older brothers, that J.T. would be just fine. He would have physical limitations, and perhaps bouts with depression, but he was no longer under doctor's care, and he seemed happy. Life on the farm seemed almost normal again.

J.T. made tremendous progress in the years following the accident. Before the age of six he was maneuvering with the one crutch in just the way his dad had envisioned. Managing steps, walking long distances, or doing his chores, he seemed to master every physical challenge. As life and energy returned to the home, there was another big change in store for J.T. and the family. J.T. would have to assume a new role; that of Big Brother! He relished the opportunity to welcome his little sister, Mable, into the family.

J.T. and Mable shared some happy times together during their pre-teen years. Stories told over the years during family reunions and other occasions reveal poignant memories too precious not to capture for future generations. A particularly heart rending story involved their mom. Lucy was not afforded the opportunity to attend school past third grade. Even so, she wanted her children to attend school and get an education. Lucy saved the tops of shoe boxes. On those cardboard boxes, she took a grease pencil and wrote the alphabet on one and numbers from one to one hundred on others. On Sundays after Church she would teach her children their numbers, and how to write their names.

When J.T. and Mable were finally able to attend school, they had already been taught to write their names, and count to one hundred. J.T. and Mable also recalled their mom, Lucy, kneeling beside them at night and teaching them the Lord's Prayer. She patiently repeated the process each night until they memorized the passage and could utter the prayer themselves.

Educational pursuits were not as important to J.T.'s dad. Willis could not read or write. When official signatures were required, he would formalize a document with his mark, or attempt to scratch out his name to the best of his ability. His chief concern was the work on the farm, which was the family's livelihood. Besides, who would take J.T. to school, and bring him home?

His older brothers were no longer in school. No one in the family to that point had even finished high school. Perhaps Willis thought that farming didn't require book learning, just experience.

So J.T. was not allowed to attend school until he was nine years old. He started school three years behind his classmates.

Chapter Six

KIDS WILL BE KIDS

Whether it's 1940 or 1840, kids will be kids. J.T. and Mable were the middle children of the family. They were the closest in age, and over the years they shared many stories about growing up as the children of sharecroppers. They were born into extreme poverty. As black children growing up in the late 1930's, their life expectancy was nearly 10 years below that of white children. Luckily, these two blessed children didn't grow up feeling sorry for themselves. They were gifted, strong willed, and longed to do the same thing any kid in America would do; have fun!

Saturday's were usually rest days on the farm. On Saturday's, twice a month, Willis and Lucy would go into town and shop for supplies. Most of the time Lucy and Willis would take a buck board wagon, pulled by one of Willis' two mules, Maggie or Sam. Other times they'd get a ride from a friend, or the landowner.

The children looked forward to those Saturday's. Lucy would always return with a giant peppermint stick, a block of hoop cheese, and a box of vanilla wafers, for the children. The children loved to snack on the hoop cheese sandwiched between saltine crackers, or vanilla wafers. Throughout the week, Lucy would treat her children to blocks of candy from the giant peppermint stick.

When the parents were away on Saturday's, J.T. was often left in charge as the oldest child at home. His big brothers, Willis III (Poodah) and John (Boo), were older teenagers who were busy with their own activities. This would often leave J.T. and Mable home alone. With no television, video games, or play grounds available, what would they do for fun? I'm glad you asked. How about a game of chicken? Not at all the chicken you might be envisioning. Chicken was a standard entrée in the south; fried, baked, broiled, pit barbeque, you name it. Willis raised chickens by the dozens.

Preparing the chicken on some small farms in those days was a crude sight to behold. The process gave birth to the southern euphemism, "running around like a chicken with your head cut off." The children were taken aback at the sight of Willis beginning the process.

First, he would single out a chicken and place it separately in a coop for three days. The chicken would be fed a steady diet of corn. At the end of three days the chicken would be bulging and ready for slaughter. Willis would grab the chicken by its head, and in a circular motion make three turns and snap...holding the head in his hand, as the chicken ran aimlessly for about a minute until it collapsed. Then it was hot water to remove the feathers and so on…

Well, J.T. and Mable had watched this process for quite a while. They also loved fried chicken. So, on some Saturday's when Willis and Lucy left to go into town, J.T. and Mable would prepare a bird, and treat themselves to fried chicken for lunch. J.T., always watching and trying to emulate his dad, would do the ringing and cleaning. Mable, who was a quick understudy of her mom, would cut the chicken into parts, and do the frying. Mable also recalled J.T.'s first exploits at shaving, long before he'd grown any facial hair! J.T. would get his dad's shaving equipment, which consisted of a mug, shaving brush, and soap. He'd lather up his face, and do his best impersonation of his dad's shaving technique. This impersonation included humming and miming his daddy's favorite blues or country and western tune.

The two of them shared these stories at a family reunion in Detroit in the summer of 2009. A group of us listened intently, and hung on every word. We all laughed for quite a while…

Chapter Seven

MISCHIEVOUS

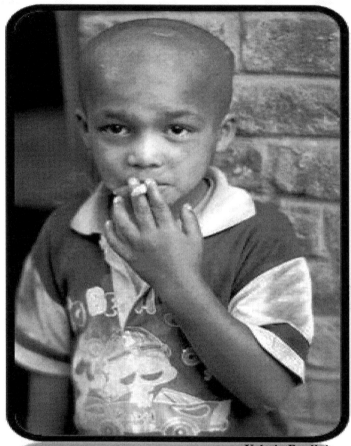

Valerio Berdini
Photography

According to J.T.'s mom, Lucy, his big brothers and other close relatives, J.T. was not expected to have a long life. In the early months following the accident, his dad would place him in the middle of the table during dinner, allowing J.T. to be the center of attention. Even when it became clear that J.T. would not only survive, but thrive, Willis would not allow him to be disciplined in any physical manner, as had been the case with the earlier children. Some of J.T.'s siblings would later comment that J.T. was "spoiled," or given preferential treatment by his dad. If this was the case, perhaps it was because of Willis' gratitude and relief that his little son had survived a brush with death. Maybe little J.T. was a miracle to him. In a hard scrabble life in which nothing came easy, J.T. defied the odds and was a source of constant inspiration.

As J.T. came of age, he grew adept at leveraging his get out of jail free card. He would misbehave from time to time in the home and in the community, but he always seemed to escape serious discipline or detention. Some of J.T.'s own stories are incredible, and remarkably candid.

As discussed earlier, J.T. emulated his dad in many ways. Most notably in his work ethic and the skill in which he dispensed his duties on the farm. But there were other ways in which he experimented at a very young age that were not so healthy. Willis Martin and his brothers were hard drinkers. During Prohibition, they made Moonshine Whiskey back in Alabama. They did not lose the recipe when they moved to Louisiana.

J.T. watched his dad and other men socialize and drink corn whiskey or "white Lightning"… straight from the jug. J.T. vividly tells the story of taking a "swig" of his dad's whiskey on a few occasions. J.T. doesn't remember the exact age he took his first swig. But he did remember "having to lean that jug to the side because it was too heavy to lift."

J.T. recalls smoking his first filtered cigarette when he was about 6 years old. One day, J.T. observed one of the town's wealthy landowners in a conversation with his dad. J.T. recalled, "The man pulled out a pack of Lucky Strike cigarettes and lit up a smoke." It was a filtered cigarette and that was new to J.T., who had observed his dad smoking the Prince Albert variety, where one had to pour tobacco into leafy paper filters and roll it. Curious and not afraid to engage with adults, J.T. asked the man for a cigarette. The man turned to J.T.'s dad and said, "Is it alright, Willis?" Willis nodded and said, "Yassa, it's okay." The man gave J.T. the rest of the pack. According to J.T.'s recollection of the transfer, "a little less than half the pack remained." When the conversation ended and the man left, Willis immediately commandeered the cigarettes from J.T.

He would smoke Lucky Strike for the rest of the day and not the usual "poor man" Prince Albert brand. In the months and years to come, nearly every time the man saw J.T., he'd give him cigarettes. These innocent gifts of transfer began a habit that J.T. would indulge in for nearly 60 years.

Chapter Eight

LIFE AS A SHARECROPPER'S SON

Life on the farm was fun, as J.T. recalled, "We had some good times." In recounting stories of his youth J.T. never complained about the work, or his lot in life. As J.T. matured into his teen years, it became evident that even with the loss of his leg, he would be tall and lean, likely over six feet. Talented and athletic, he willed himself to compete physically with his peers. Many years later his contemporaries described him as a physical marvel, never held back by handicap. He didn't spend time feeling sorry for himself. He climbed trees, played marbles, and sometimes jumped rope with the girls.

There was a pond on the farm where the cattle often drank. The family members would take a dip in the cool waters during the summer months. J.T. was proud of the fact that he taught himself to swim in that pond. A fact that was validated by Mable and Poodah in many stories over the years.

J.T. settled into a good rhythm of work around the farm. He established himself as a hard worker and a quick study. J.T. was remarkable at learning the tricks of the trade by observation. He mastered the art of hoeing cotton by watching his dad. He mastered the art of picking cotton by observing a man named

"Cotton-Picking Mose," who J.T. recalls as the best cotton picker in the area. Almost like poetry, he described how Mose would "pop his burlap cotton sack and glide down the rows, using both hands to pluck the cotton from the bolls." He emulated Mose's style and technique, and as he physically matured, he mastered the art of cotton picking.

In the evenings after work the family would settle in and relax after dinner. There was no television for entertainment, and the radio reception was poor. The children would play cards, dominoes, or checkers. When family members visited, adults would share stories. J.T.'s dad was a great story teller, and J.T. loved to listen to his funny stories and colorful jokes. J.T. enjoyed when the family would visit Willis' brother, Uncle Bob, who they affectionately called, "Two Man." The story goes that Bob Martin was an excellent wrestler. A real "tough son of a gun." In fact, the legend goes that Bob could never be wrestled to the ground by one man. It took at least two. Hence, the nick name, "Two Man." Uncle Bob had a radio with decent reception, so it was nice to be able to listen to music, radio programs, and hear news about the world outside of the farm.

One of the really neat things he enjoyed doing was going to the "Picture Show," or movies as its most often called today. J.T. recalls his brother, Poodah, accompanying him to see his first movie, "probably in the late 1930's." The price of admission was "a dime for the movie and a nickel for popcorn." J.T. loved the westerns, and became a big fan of stars like, "Roy Rogers, Gene Autry, and Buck Jones." Like restaurants, bathrooms, and other public places in those days, the movie theater was segregated. black patrons sat upstairs in the balcony.

J.T. never wanted to be marginalized. He watched his older brothers do their chores and he tried to emulate them. There were plenty of chores to do on the farm. The family raised chickens, pigs, and they always had a cow for milk and butter. With his older brothers working in the cotton fields alongside his dad, J.T. assumed the duties of feeding, watering, and tending to the animals. He also learned to milk cows and churn butter.

Mastering the chores around the house was not enough for J.T. He was older now and he handled himself quite well. He wanted to contribute more. He was not content to use his handicap to avoid hard work. One of his responsibilities was to carry water out to his dad and others who were removing grass and weeds from cotton plants with a hoe. J.T. had long watched his dad and mom hoe cotton. He had even practiced, learning how to balance and position himself along the rows. He longed for the time when his dad would recognize his ability to do the work and allow him to join the adults.

J.T. had an idea. The rows of cotton sometimes stretched for half a mile. J.T. would wait until the group neared the far end of the field. Then he would begin hoeing their return rows. About ten yards for each row, enough for the adults to notice as they approached the end. When the adults returned, some wondered aloud who had finished out their row, and how well it looked. Willis looked over with pride at J.T. He knew J.T. had done the work.

The very next week, Willis allowed J.T. to join his mom, Lucy, and a team of ladies who were hoeing cotton separately from the men (women's wages were significantly lower). At eleven years of age, J.T. was working in the cotton fields with adult female sharecroppers, and holding his own. J.T. recalled that the adult male wage was one dollar per day, and the female wage was fifty cents per day. He longed to work his way into the adult male rotation so he could double his pay!

Chapter Nine

THAT A BOY, SHEP!

According to J.T. and other members of his family, Shep was simply the best coon dog in the state of Louisiana. Shep could "tree a coon like no other dog we ever had or saw." Raccoon meat was a staple for the family. Willis would clean the animal and remove the insides, similar to the manner in which they cleaned a chicken. Lucy would then boil it to "get rid of the wildness and gamey taste." Finally, she would bake the animal, often with sweet potatoes or white potatoes on the side.

So for over a decade, Shep had been an integral part of the family; he was a loyal watch dog, a happy playmate for J.T. and Mable, and an excellent hunting partner for Willis and his older sons. And who in the family would ever forget that it was Shep who first alerted men at the sawmill with his fierce barking after J.T.'s tragic accident, perhaps saving his life on that day.

At 88 years of age, J.T. recalls the events surrounding Shep's death. Shep was getting on in years but he was still feisty. He was still an able hunting partner, and most often the coon hunting occurred at night. During one cotton season in the late 1930's, there was a devastating boll weevil outbreak. J.T. recalls that he and Poodah were given the task of spraying what would be considered a strong insecticide on the cotton plants. This insecticide was dispensed by a hand carried machine using a circular motion. The boys wore masks due to the toxicity of the insecticide. This operation was carried out at night to maximize its effectiveness…"the dew would help to ensure the insecticide would cling to the cotton plants."

As he would often do, Shep followed J.T. and Poodah on their mission. It didn't immediately occur to the boys that ole Shep might be impacted by the toxic spray. Shep would show no immediate reaction to the insecticide. But after a few days he started to lie around more and become lethargic. He stopped eating, and his bark sounded more like a cry for help. It finally dawned on the boys, and Willis, that Shep had likely breathed in a lethal dose of the toxic insecticide. After a few days Shep would die in his sleep overnight; the first member of the family to die who made the trip from Alabama. J.T. remembers how sad he was at his passing. They buried ole Shep on the property near their sharecropper's home. For a long time, there was a grave marker at the little burial site emblazoned with his name.

Chapter Ten

STRIPES...

Over my half century of life, I've heard many stories from my dad, uncles, cousins, and family friends, regarding the farming exploits of Willis Martin, Sr. Many lauded his ability to set a plow and cultivate fields, train mules and care for farm animals. According to J.T. and Poodah, there was not much on a farm Willis wasn't good at. The landowner Willis farmed for shared those sentiments. With J.T.'s accident being a very notable exception, the first decade of the Martin's move to Louisiana had been productive, even prosperous for the landowner.

Despite what one would have called a mutually beneficial relationship between Willis and the landowner, there was one glaring issue. Willis was a heavy drinker, and sometimes his drinking impeded his work. He learned how to make white Lightning (corn whiskey) back home in Alabama, while watching his relatives mix the sinus clearing brew in back wood Stills. He continued the process in Louisiana, and always kept a jug of whiskey around the house.

Although he knew how to operate a vehicle, Willis did not own one during most of his time working as a sharecropper in Louisiana. He could use the landowner's truck as required to drive into town and pick up farm supplies, and to buy groceries for his family on occasion. This was a privilege Willis began to abuse due to excessive drinking. According to stories, he was stopped by police on multiple occasions due to weaving and swerving, as he tried to operate a sluggish steering farm vehicle on uneven roads while impaired.

Due to the landowners standing in the community (he also happened to be a lawyer), the first couple of incidents resulted in Willis receiving a stern warning. Many years later, a colorful accounting from Poodah, revealed that Willis did not immediately discontinue the practice of drinking and driving. The landowner was very vocal with Willis. He'd had enough with Willis' lack of discipline and disregard for his authority and guidance. J.T. and Poodah would recall many years later that this incident had so roiled the landowner that Willis knew he'd crossed a line. He knew he had to take immediate steps to atone for his actions and regain the confidence of the landowner. So, Willis did something that his wife or children never saw him do before. "He got religion." To get out of the landowner's doghouse, Willis got baptized in a lake called, Providence, and he made sure the landowner knew about it.

Willis managed to toe the line for several months, but unfortunately, he had another incident with alcohol impaired driving. The landowner was furious and was in no mood for excuses. He refused to bail Willis out of jail. Willis was sentenced to 90 days at a prison farm in East Carroll Parish Louisiana. The prison farm was not a maximum-security facility. It was a minimum security correctional facility where penal labor convicts were put to economical use such as farming or logging.

J.T. recalls the family visiting his dad in the prison on a weekend. His mom packed food for the 10-mile trip, and Poodah drove the wagon. They spent a few hours at the penal farm, careful to leave in time to get the mule team home before dark. Willis was able to casually visit and share a meal with his family.

What did the children think when they visited their dad at the prison farm? There were questions to their mom, Lucy, about why their dad could not come home with them. It was a day that J.T. never forgot. He still remembers Poodah driving away, and his dad standing at the fence and waving until the wagon rolled around the bend and out of sight.

Poodah assumed the leadership role of managing the farm work during his dad's 90-day absence. J.T. was ready, and stepped up to assume greater responsibility.

Chapter Eleven

THE THREE R'S

For sharecroppers in the Deep South during the Great Depression years of the 1930s and 40s, farming was king. Many youngsters attended school only 5 or 6 months of the year due to planting and harvesting priorities on the farm. Farming was often a family affair. All hands-on deck to get crops planted in the spring, and to get the cotton, sweet potatoes, and other crops harvested in late summer through early fall. Such was the case with J.T., and his sister, Mable.

Although school was not a priority for J.T.'s dad, he allowed J.T. and Mable to attend, when farming duties were not required. J.T. and Mable both loved school. They had very fond recollections of their elementary and high school years of schooling. When asked about their affinity for school they offered several interesting reasons.

Their mom's early instruction of the alphabet and numbers on the back of the shoe boxes had whet their appetites for learning. From time to time as children "they'd see a newspaper or picture book, and longed to be able to read the writings which described the pictures."

They also viewed the opportunity to attend school as a social event. A time they could look forward to leaving the farm and their house, which was located in a field that offered a close up view of cotton stalks on either side.

The first school they attended was housed in a Methodist church. The same church they attended for Sunday services. The school had one room, one teacher, and 20-25 students of various ages. But it didn't matter to the children. It was a welcome respite from the farm. They were able to learn new things, and socialize and expand their network of friends in the community.

The learning environment at the school was not ideal. Forty years earlier the landmark U.S. Supreme Court case, "Plessy v. Ferguson" (1896), upheld state racial segregation laws for public facilities under the doctrine of separate but equal. Conditions at the all black school were far from equal. But despite substandard conditions, outdated and worn textbooks, and desks handed down from the all-white schools, the children learned.

Reading, writing, and arithmetic, were the basic staples of education taught at the school. The school teacher was dedicated, and it helped that she was providing instruction to a class of students with a passion for learning. Discipline was not a problem. The teacher had the authority to paddle those who presented a disciplinary problem. According to J.T., double jeopardy was authorized. "If you got your back side tanned at school and your parents found out about it, it's a good chance you'd receive another lickin' when you got home."

Within a couple of years J.T. was reading at a high level. He recalls being very proud of reading in Church for the first time in front of his mom. He quickly excelled in arithmetic, and recalled with pride how he had sometimes assisted his dad in calculating poundage for cotton bales during harvest season, and writing it out legibly for the record.

Chapter Twelve

LEAD WOOD

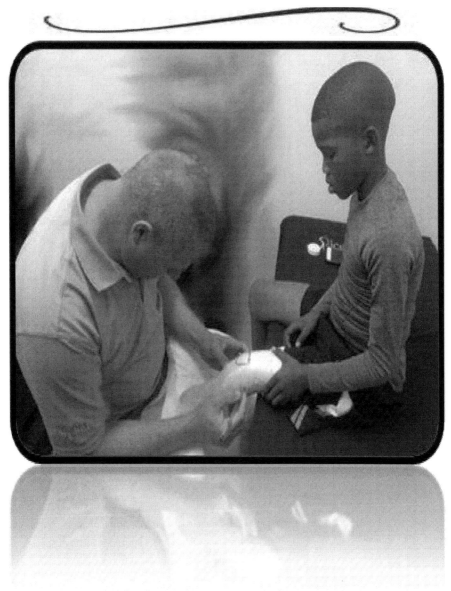

J.T. progressed nicely through his first years of school. Utilizing one crutch, he was able to keep up with Mable for the one mile trek each morning. He wore jeans or khakis everyday just like the other boys. J.T. would simply take the pant leg from his missing limb and tuck it in his pocket. J.T. recalls "somewhere around 5th or 6th grade, his mom received notification from the state health office regarding J.T.'s eligibility for a prosthesis at no expense, due to his disability. Neither J.T. nor his mom knew much about the process, but were eager to learn more.

The evaluation for J.T.'s prosthesis was 60 miles away in Monroe, Louisiana. It would be J.T.'s first long distance trip away from home. As the time drew near for the trip J.T. could hardly contain his excitement. His thoughts were racing about the prospect of a prosthesis. Would it make it even easier for him to walk, or maybe even run a bit? Now he might no longer have to tuck the dangling pant leg in his pocket.

They were up early on the morning of the evaluation. His mom packed salt meat sandwiches and vanilla wafers for the trip. J.T. was excited about his first real trip out of the Parish, but even more intrigued to experience the prosthesis evaluation. They departed for Monroe after first light.

According to the Monroe News-Star newspaper, the population of Monroe, La., in 1940 was just under 30,000 people. As they drove into the city and made their way to the medical facility, J.T. recalls "it was the most people I'd ever seen in one place."

J.T. and his mom walked into the facility and checked in at the front desk. They took a seat in the waiting area. J.T. started to fidget a bit. He didn't want to worry his mom but he needed to relieve himself. He recalled entering the facility from the parking lot area, and he didn't recall seeing an outhouse. Finally, when he felt he could wait no longer, he whispered to his mom that he really needed to go outside and find a place to relieve himself. His mom was very understanding. She thoughtfully approached the nice lady at the desk and asked for the location of the nearest facility.

She pointed down the hallway just a short distance from where they were sitting. J.T. followed his mom down the hallway and saw a door marked for "Men." He opened the door and looked in. There inside was a toilet and a urinal. It marked the first time in J.T.'s young life that he would use indoor plumbing. It would be seven years before he would use an indoor toilet on a regular basis again.

Shortly after returning to his seat his name was called for the evaluation. The doctor was very nice. As the examination began, the doctor paused as he gazed upon J.T.'s missing leg. J.T. only had 6 inches of leg remaining after the accident. The doctor who performed the surgery after the accident was very concerned about infection, so to be on the safe side he removed nearly all of little J.T.'s leg. The remaining six inches would make the prosthesis adjustment more difficult.

The prosthesis was not what J.T. had envisioned. Unlike today's modern equipment being fitted for our troops, and other individuals who suffer the loss of a limb, the 1940's prosthesis was a heavy wooden apparatus, shaped like a leg, but bulky and cumbersome. It gave a semblance of normalcy from a standing position. But walking proved challenging.

J.T. was fitted for the prosthesis, and used it from time to time. But most often he just utilized old faithful, the one custom made, oak hewn crutch, which had served him so well.

Chapter Thirteen

MY BROTHER, MY FRIEND

J.T. was remarkably adjusted and confident as he approached his teenage years. The farm work was going well for him. His work ethic and skill in the cotton fields had resulted in him being elevated to work along with his dad and the adult crews.

His brother, Poodah, was instrumental in J.T.'s development as a skillful worker. Poodah took a very patient, hands-on approach to train his younger brother, and J.T. heeded every word. Poodah had established a great relationship with the landowner, who was very impressed and pleased with Poodah's work.

The landowner had always been very sensitive regarding J.T.'s tragic accident which occurred near his property a decade earlier. He closely tracked J.T.'s progress over the years. He marveled at J.T.'s resiliency and outstanding physical capabilities, which propelled him as a teenager to do the work of an adult, despite having a missing leg. J.T. and the landowner developed a close personal relationship.

As J.T. neared his teen years he recalled that his relationship and bond with his older brother, Poodah, became increasingly strong. Poodah was a sensitive young man by this time. He loved J.T., and had always taken a special interest in his well-being. Poodah wasn't home on the fateful morning of J.T.'s accident, but when he returned and saw his little brother, he cried for hours. J.T. would have a special place in Poodah's heart for life.

J.T. initially inherited Poodah's chores around the farm. It was Poodah who taught him how to milk a cow, and feed the farm animals. They bunked in the same room. Poodah once commented to J.T. later in life. "Do you remember anything about that old house we lived in when Daddy was sharecropping?" "Yeah, I remember a lot about that house," J.T. said. Caught up in laughter, Poodah replied, "Boy we could lay down at night and see the stars, and look down through the floor and see the chickens running under the house."

On another occasion Poodah recalls a time when J.T. was about 8 or 9 years old. Their paternal grandmother, Viola, was on an extended visit from Alabama. One evening, Viola made a batch of tea cakes. Even though they are called cakes, tea cakes are just old fashioned cookies made with butter, sugar, eggs, and lemon or vanilla extract. They are delicious!

At any rate, Ms. Viola planned to let the tea cakes cool and sit overnight, and serve them the following day during lunch and dinner. The smell of the tea cakes was just too overwhelming for Poodah and J.T. With Ms. Viola resting in a room adjacent to the kitchen, they had to devise a plan to distract her in order to pilfer a few tea cakes for a nighttime snack. Big brother Poodah came up with the plan. "Okay now listen J.T.," he whispered. "I'mma strike up a conversation with Grandma, and you sneak in there in the kitchen and get us a few of them tea cakes." "Okay Poodah I'll do it," J.T. said. So while Poodah conversed with his poor, unsuspecting, Grandma Viola, little J.T. was low crawling past her room on the floor to the kitchen. He snagged four tea cakes, neatly placed the foil back around the container, and Grandma never suspected a thing.

Poodah recalls a poignant memory that he and J.T. shared on a warm summer afternoon in the early 1940's. Poodah was about 18 or 19 at the time. He had been plowing for most of the day, and J.T. had come over to bring him water. "J.T. let's sit a spell, I need to tell you something." J.T. was happy to sit and talk with his older brother. He would always hang on his every word. "J.T. I need to tell you something. I ain't even told Dad yet, but I'm telling you now. I'mma 'bout to leave the farm." In a breath J.T. replied, "Where ya going Poodah and how long you gonna be gone?" Poodah (who would live to be 97 years old) became emotional when he answered his little brother. "I'm a man now, and it's time for me to go and make my own way." J.T. paused, never taking his eyes off Poodah. "Don't leave me Poodah, don't go. I'll miss you Poodah, don't go…"

Chapter Fourteen

A HOUSE DIVIDED

As J.T. approached his teen years, in many ways he still exhibited that remarkable resiliency, which inspired so many people in the community who knew his life story. He continued to defy the odds and overcome almost any physical obstacle. Aside from the loss of his leg, he was a well-built youngster with no other physical maladies. He had better than average height for his age, and a smooth lean athletic frame.

After Poodah's departure, J.T. assumed a larger role on the farm. He grew closer to the owner, who entrusted him with greater responsibility. J.T. was now working with the adult men. He needed no assistance. He held his own, and then some, whether chopping or picking cotton, or any other work on the farm. He had a great attitude about work. His handicap did not define him. He was defined and respected by his work ethic and skill.

The family seemed to be settled again after Poodah's departure. The house was smaller now with the arrival of two more children. Mable had a job babysitting for the family that owned the local drug store. When she was not working in the fields or caring for her children, Lucy had part time work cleaning homes and washing clothes for wealthy white people in the community.

Despite the growth and maturity of J.T. and his sister, Mable, and the hard work and loyalty of their mom, Lucy, something dreadful was stirring in the home.

After over a decade on the farm, Willis was restless. Although his time on the farm was productive, his night life and extracurricular activities prohibited him from saving much money or raising the family's standard of living. As J.T. and the younger children matured they became concerned and sometimes vocal about their dad's blatant disrespect for their mom. Outside of work, the once harmonious home life was rapidly deteriorating into a climate of constant verbal abuse.

Without much discussion or emotion, Willis made the decision to leave his family, and leave the farm. The only life J.T. had known was coming to an immediate end. His dad, the one who he'd always tried to please and impress, was leaving his family without a reasonable explanation.

Years later J.T. and Mable would comment that they were not saddened, but relieved at their dad's departure. The children coalesced around their mom, and she provided the consistent leadership and stability the family would require to succeed in a very challenging environment. Each of the four children she raised alone after the separation were high school graduates.

Chapter Fifteen

MAN OF THE HOUSE

In just a matter of a couple of years, J.T. endured the departure of his dad, and Poodah, his beloved brother and confidant. This would have been an overwhelmingly emotional event for any ordinary boy to undergo, let alone one who had experienced the challenges J.T. had. Poodah's departure happened over the course of time, in keeping with the circle of life. But his dad's departure as the head of the family was unexpected and alarming.

As a result of his dad's departure, J.T.'s mom, Lucy, moved with her four children away from the sharecropper tenant quarters. Lucy was a conservative and frugal money manager. She didn't drink or smoke. She fancied a little Bitter Garrett snuff in the evenings. She had managed to tuck away enough money over the years to afford a deposit on a small rental house closer to town. There was no indoor plumbing, so the family still had to endure the dreaded outhouse. There was no bathtub or shower facility. Baths were done in a wash tub. The house had few amenities, but it was serviceable, and the family was together, and safe.

Over the course of his young life, J.T. had met every challenge thrown his way. He had a good sense of humor, always positive, and he rarely cried. He loved his mom. When his dad left the family, he didn't need a pep talk. He knew it was his place to support his mom and his younger siblings.

And so now here was J.T., barely a teenager. The little boy who endured a horrific accident, and who many thought would die, would now be called upon to shoulder a load no teenager should have to bear. By this point, Lucy didn't treat him with kid gloves. Not only had God spared her son's life, he'd blessed him with extraordinary courage and an indomitable spirit.

Lucy worked in town as a domestic for a man who ran the post office. She kept his house cleaned and washed his clothes. She also made extra money for the family during the pipeline season. Oil and Natural Gas pipeline crews often stopped through the area. Lucy would wash clothes for the crew. J.T. and Mable helped their mom every step of the way. J.T. would light a fire under a big cast iron vat, and they would use lye soap to hand scrub the clothes and hang them out on a close line to dry.

In addition to helping his mom with the pipeline crews, J.T. continued to do farm work. Although they no longer lived on the sharecropper farm, J.T. maintained a good relationship with the landowner. He continued to do part-time work helping with the cattle and in the fields.

J.T. recalls with excitement when a new farmer came to the area from Memphis, Tennessee. J.T. jumped at the chance to work for this gentleman because he paid a daily, sun up to sun down wage of $2! A 100 percent pay increase for J.T., as the mid-1940's approached, and the country slowly but steadily climbed out of the Great Depression.

He recalls working in the fields in those days with a song in his heart, and on his lips. When asked, what songs did he sing, he hummed a few bars of a song called, "There's a Star-Spangled Banner Waving Somewhere." A quick google search revealed that the song was recorded in 1942 (during WWII) by country music artist Elton Britt. Not able to serve in the military due to his handicap, perhaps J.T. was drawn to this passage, "Though I realize I am crippled, that is true sir, please don't judge my courage by my twisted leg, let me show my Uncle Sam what I can do, sir, let me help to bring the axis down a peg."

J.T. fondly recalls picking cotton. He boasted about being one of the highest earners each time out, by virtue of picking more pounds of cotton than anyone else during the course of a day. He loved to get out and start early. J.T. explained that "the early morning dew would make the cotton heavier, and my first bag would easily be over 50 pounds." Over the years, he'd cheerfully explain his technique and how he was able to maneuver through the fields with the one crutch, and still always "pick a clean row of cotton." He was proud of that.

He beamed with pride as he recalled one extraordinary day in the cotton field. J.T. got off to an early start and he had a great day picking cotton. He always worked hard because he knew how much his mom and siblings depended on his income to support the family. But this was an exceptional day. By the end of the day J.T. had picked over 300 pounds of cotton. The pay line was slow that evening, and J.T. was in a rush to get home. He asked an honest married couple, who happened to be good friends of his mom's, to get his wages and he'd pick up the money later. When J.T. dropped by their house later in the evening he immediately sensed that something was wrong. The landowner had refused to give them J.T.'s wages. He didn't believe that anyone in that work crew could pick 300 pounds of cotton, and especially not a handicapped person.

J.T. didn't frown or fret. He looked them both in the eye and said, "That's okay, I'll show 'em tomorrow." Motivated to prove a point and recoup the lost day of wages, J.T. got off to a great start in the dew filled morning. Everyone on the work crew knew J.T.'s story, his work ethic, and respected him deeply. They were saddened by the fact that the landowner refused to pay his wages the day before. But they bubbled with joy at J.T.'s attitude, and the energy he displayed that day in the cotton field. The landowner had been watching during the morning hours, and he came back after lunch to witness J.T. continuing a blistering, machine like pace, in his quest to prove that he'd earned his money the day before.

Nearing the end of the day, J.T. was finishing out his last row. He was clearly ahead of everyone, and he cleanly picked the cotton out of every boll on his rows. According to J.T., and witnesses who remember the event, there were nearly 100 people cheering him on as he neared the end of the row. Some of those cheering were members of the community work crew. But many were people who the landowner had called to come and see this young handicapped black man who picks cotton like a machine.

At the end of the day, J.T. had picked more cotton than the day before. The landowner shook his head as if to marvel at J.T.'s ability. He happily gave J.T. his wages for both days.

This accomplishment gave J.T. a great deal of personal satisfaction. Once again, he'd proved that he shouldn't be judged by his handicap, but by his heart.

J.T. worked a variety of jobs to help his mom and support the family. He almost always gave his mom his entire wages (a claim that Lucy validated with pride many years later). At the end of three years, his mom had saved over $500. She hired a carpenter and had a new home constructed for the family. Still no indoor plumbing, but the family finally had a home of their own.

During a bleak period of uncertainty, J.T. had stepped up, displaying wisdom and courage which belied his years. With calm self-assurance, he helped to bring security and stability to the family, and proved to be a very able man of the house.

Chapter Sixteen

SWEET MAGNOLIA

As the mid-1940's approached, the country had begun to climb out of the grips of the Great Depression. The tide was turning for the United States, and the Allied Powers in World War II. J.T. remembers this type of information being announced at the picture show on the old Movietone News Reels. As World War II ended in 1945, J.T.'s high school experience was beginning. J.T. would attend Magnolia High School in Pioneer, Louisiana, to complete grades 9-11. J.T.'s class was the last to require completion of 11th grade for high school graduation. Thereafter, a 12th grade requirement was instituted for high school completion.

"Magnolia" was a most appropriate name for the school. It is the state flower for Louisiana. The school grounds were dotted with beautiful Magnolia trees, which boasted dark green, oval shaped leaves, seemingly covered with a layer of wax. The trees so beautifully announced the spring's annual arrival, with breath-taking pink chiffon-like blossoms.

Magnolia High School was 10 miles from J.T.'s home. His previous elementary and junior high school attendance consisted of a 1 to 2 mile walk. His high school experience would begin with his first school bus ride. J.T. and the other children enjoyed the daily trek through the country side. Their bus driver, Roosevelt Weston, was a very prominent man in the small black community, and he always had a kind word for the children each morning and afternoon.

J.T. immediately embraced the new school environment. His favorite subjects were "science and agriculture." He enjoyed field trips to local farms, which allowed him to exhibit subject matter expertise in a number of areas. He also enjoyed time in the science lab conducting experiments, dissecting frogs and the like, and learning scientific explanations for plant growth and maintaining the health of crops.

J.T. has great memories of his high school experience. He said, "Boy, we had a lot of fun!" The mischievous streak he displayed as a child followed him into high school. He recalls the first days of a new teacher, Mr. Blankenship. On his first day of school, he created a role call to establish the members of his class; he led a group of boys who decided to have a little fun with the new teacher. Mr. Blankenship called on J.T. first. "What's your name, son?" J.T said, "Roy Rogers, sir." "Okay, thank you Roy." He looked at the boys sitting next to J.T., "Your name, young man?" "Johnny Mack Brown, sir." "And yours young man?" "Gene Autry, sir." For the next couple of days, Mr. Blankenship used these names to call role. The class chuckled at how easy J.T. pulled off the prank.

About three days into the school year, the school principal, Mrs. Oliver, stopped in at the beginning of class. As Mr. Blankenship began to call roll; Roy Rogers, Gene Autry, Johnny Mack Brown... Mrs. Oliver immediately shook her head and knew that a mischievous caper had been pulled on the new teacher. For their well thought out and well executed prank, J.T. and his band of merry men were rewarded with wall washing duty during recess for the next week.

J.T. never experienced any real taunting or ridicule due to his disability. Most of his contemporaries were sensitive to his plight, and admired his toughness and strong will in overcoming adversity. However, there were a couple of new kids in high school who made disgusting jokes about his disability. They persisted in their comments, but these miscreants were careful not to do so within arm's length of J.T., who by this time was one of the largest boys in school.

J.T. was not overly sensitive, but over time he'd had his fill of these jokesters. On the bus ride home one day, he had a discussion with his cousin, George Martin. George was the fastest runner in school. "George, I've had it with these guys. I believe if I could get my hands on one of them I could stop this, but I can't catch 'em. Next time they start up I want you to grab one of them and hold 'em down till I get there okay?" George agreed.

The very next day during recess, while maintaining a safe distance, the 2 kids began to heckle J.T. George Martin lit out after one of them, tracked him down and was holding him to the ground. "Come on J.T., I can't hold 'em!" J.T. ambled over to the area, near the edge of a corn field, where George was holding down one of the now squirming jokesters. J.T. snagged a corn stalk as he got closer. "Okay George, you can let go. I got him now." J.T. proceeded to give the prankster a whipping with the corn stalk, as the other kids laughed hysterically! "Mr. J.T., I'm sorry, I didn't mean nuttin' by it!" From that day forward, J.T. no longer had to endure any pranksters at Magnolia High School.

The years flew by at Magnolia; there were fond times, happy times. J.T. recalls his senior prom, and his prom date, Velma Smith. Velma was affectionately called, "Little Honey," by her classmates. The nickname was derived from her mom, whose given name was "Honey." J.T., Johnny Smith, and a couple of other boys, had a great time at the prom. Someone had sneaked in some "white Port" wine. The boys had a real buzz as they listened to the tunes of Ray Charles, Lena Horne, Frank Sinatra and others, while keeping a safe distance from Mrs. Oliver, the school principal, and other chaperones.

Finally, it was time to graduate from good ole Magnolia High School. J.T.'s graduating class consisted of 11 students. The sponsor for J.T.'s class was a woman he admired greatly,

Lillie Beasley. Ms. Beasley taught music education. J.T. enjoyed being in her class. As part of the graduation ceremonies, Ms. Beasley announced that she was selecting a member of the graduating class to sing a solo.

None of his fellow students were surprised when Ms. Beasley selected J.T. to sing the solo at the graduation ceremony. J.T. had a beautiful voice. Ms. Beasley selected the song, "Oh Danny Boy," and she accompanied him on the piano. J.T.'s mom was there for the ceremony, and so was his sister, Mable. J.T. recalls being nervous before the performance, but he sang wonderfully, and received a standing ovation from his classmates and members of the audience. Ms. Beasley beamed with pride.

It was a wonderful day for J.T.'s mom, Lucy. She was filled with pride as she listened to her son sing so wonderfully, and be so well received by the audience and his classmates. Perhaps her thoughts drifted back to the early days, of teaching her children their numbers and alphabets on the back of shoe boxes. Or maybe even farther, when she wondered if her little J.T. could ever experience any semblance of a normal life. Once again, J.T. had exceeded expectations. He had completed his high school experience on a high note! It was a blessed day!

Chapter Seventeen

THE GREAT MIGRATION... MINUS ONE

With Magnolia High School now in his rear view mirror, what would the future hold for J.T.? There was very little industrial or factory type opportunities in the area. With his disability, military service was not an option. He knew of friends and family members who were a part of the Great Migration of blacks who left the rural south in the first half of the 19th century, to escape oppressive economic conditions, and search for a better life in the north and west.

Given the options, J.T. seemed destined for a life in the farm industry. The landowner who the family originally sharecropped for was an admirer of J.T.'s work ethic and perseverance. He offered J.T. a position on the farm which would eventually lead to some type of management opportunity. J.T. had great respect for the landowner, and he gave serious consideration to his offer. "I was young, and I longed to see the world beyond the farm," J.T. commented.

He knew of friends and family who'd left the farm and migrated out west to Denver, Colorado. On a visit to Oak Grove, one of those friends, John Walker, described Denver in a way that peaked J.T.'s interest. He convinced J.T. they he could help him find steady employment in Denver, and a better way of life. J.T. was intrigued and longed to see the bright lights of the big city.

J.T. explained to his mom that he wanted to visit out west and pursue job prospects. To bolster his argument, he promised that after he found work he'd send money home to help care for her and his siblings. Lucy did not doubt his intentions. J.T. had always given her most of his wages for the farm work and other odd jobs he worked in the community. Her main concern was not having his strong presence in the home. She also worried about him being in the city and away from immediate family for the first time.

After careful consideration, he made the decision to make the trip to Denver. Leaving his mom and siblings was tough, but he convinced himself that it would be worth it. He'd find a job that paid good wages, and he'd be able to provide more money than ever before to help care for his family.

J.T. was excited about the road trip to Denver. His mom packed sandwiches and fried chicken for the trip. This would enable the guys to drive straight through, only having to stop for gas or bathroom breaks. In 1946, the option to stay at a motel or use the restroom was not always available for blacks.

They finally arrived in Denver in the evening near dusk. The skyline and the bright lights were everything John had described. Though tired and nearly exhausted, J.T. could hardly contain his excitement as they drove through the city. As they continued to make their way through the city, the big buildings and bright lights gave way to a less appealing part of town. It seemed to be an area inhabited by mostly black people.

After a short while they arrived at John's place, which was essentially, tenement housing. According to J.T., he was not overly impressed with his new living arrangements. He was still excited, however, at the prospect of finding good employment in Denver, enjoying the city life, and being able to send money back home to his family.

It didn't take long for J.T. to realize that some of the stories he'd heard about the big city might have been embellished a bit. The area where John lived would be characterized today as a low-income neighborhood. John was honest in his claim about his hourly salary, which was much more than he and J.T. made on the farm back home. What he failed to capture in his description of life in the big city, was the cost of living. The money John had to pay for rent, utilities, food, and the upkeep of his vehicle, really took a bite out of his weekly wages.

John took J.T. around and helped him look for work. It seems the jobs were not quite as plentiful as John claimed. Although it's possible J.T.'s handicap might have also been a factor. Finally, J.T. found a job as a fry-cook. He actually made more money in a 5-day week than he'd made in a month down south on the farm. But by the time he pitched in for rent and meals, he didn't have a lot left to send home.

True to character, J.T. kept a positive attitude. He enjoyed aspects of being in the city. He was a young man now, "fending for himself, working, paying rent and making his own way in the city." The Denver experience had taught J.T. a lot. He learned that he could take care of himself, even in an austere environment.

He also stayed true to himself and his Christian roots. He made friends in Denver, because they were drawn to the same work ethic and attitude which ingratiated him to his friends in Louisiana. After a year, though, he started to have second thoughts about city life. He missed his family, the simpler way of life, he missed home.

After 2 winters in Denver he'd made up his mind. He wanted to return home. He had dreams of going to college and getting an education. Life in the big city had been an education all its own. He called his mom and told her he was thinking about coming home. J.T. never forgot the conversation. "Mama, I'm doing okay here, but I think I want to come home." To which his mom replied, "Come on home, son, we miss you, come on home."

Chapter Eighteen

BECOMING A TIGER

J.T. was welcomed home with open arms upon his return from Denver. His mom was so happy to see him! She cooked his favorite meal, "Pinto beans, ham hocks, and hot water cornbread."

J.T. discussed his dream of going to college with his mom. Lucy was supportive of her son, now nearly 20 years old, and at a crossroads in his young life. Although she worked and saved, she didn't have the kind of money it took to send a kid to college, and there had been no formal child support coming from the children's dad.

By the grace of God, several weeks after J.T.'s return, they received a visit. Lucy recalled the visit nearly 35 years later at a Church event (which I personally attended). In her recollection of the visit, Lucy stood and offered this testimony, "A nice white feller from the government came to the house one day. He told us the government would send J.T. to school on a scholarship program cause of his disability and that we wouldn't have to pay nuttin. I thought that was a blessing, and I said, thank you, Jesus! We had been worrying and praying about how we was gonna raise the money for him to go to college. Our prayers were answered."

With no intention of attending college outside the state, there were only a few realistic choices for J.T. By law most southern colleges were still segregated in 1948. J.T. narrowed his choices to two very popular and outstanding historically black colleges; Southern University of Baton Rouge, Louisiana, and Grambling College, located about 35 miles west of Monroe, Louisiana.

J.T. was encouraged to attend Grambling by several teachers in the community who were Grambling graduates. Grambling had also been in the news of late. Earlier in 1948, Grambling's All-American football standout, Paul "Tank" Younger, was drafted by the Los Angeles Rams. He became the first athlete from a predominately black college to play in the National Football League. Legendary Coach Eddie Robinson continued to run a successful football program. But the final factor which weighed heavily in J.T.'s decision making was that Grambling was closer to home. After careful deliberation, he chose Grambling. He would be a Grambling College Tiger!

Chapter Nineteen

G-MAN

J.T. arrived at Grambling College in the fall of 1948. He was somewhat surprised to find a very quaint small town atmosphere which bordered the college. As J.T. recalled many years later, "the campus was not intimidating. It had a hometown feel from the start."

The administrators were friendly and very helpful. After getting checked in, J.T. was assigned a dorm room, and given a ride to his new home. After checking in with the dorm monitor, he was given a briefing and a nickel tour of the dormitory. About midway through the tour he was almost floored as they entered a bathroom facility. The room was equipped with several showers, toilets, and urinals. After leaving Denver and returning home, he had to adjust to outhouses again. Now, he was pleasantly surprised to learn that a significant amenity of his college experience would be indoor plumbing.

He was introduced to his two roommates; both were in their junior year of college. His new mates were very nice, and went out of their way to make J.T. feel at home in his new environment. One in particular was a guy named, "Lujack, from Chicago, Illinois." He and J.T. became fast friends. They were of similar height and build. Lujack was a snappy dresser with quite a wardrobe. "He had many of the latest styles from the city." In a wonderful gesture of kindness, he opened up his closet to J.T., and allowed him to borrow an outfit whenever he needed.

J.T. adjusted quickly to his new environment. He took a basic load of classes; math, English, psychology, and humanities. His roommates, instructors, and school officials were impressed at his ability to navigate the hilly terrain at Grambling with his disability, while utilizing only one crutch. For J.T. it was not a problem. "Every day I would strap on my backpack like a soldier and head out to class. After a few weeks, I fell into a good routine, and that's all she wrote. I remember thinking to myself; this backpack is a helluva lot lighter than a wet cotton sack."

Chapter Twenty

BY GREYHOUND OR THUMB

J.T. did not own a vehicle during his college years. During holidays, long weekends, and semester breaks, he'd have to make the 100-mile trip home by bus, or more often, to save money, by hitch-hiking.

God's favor was on him. After a few times riding the bus on Friday's the bus driver noticed there was often no one at the station to pick him up. He'd also observe J.T. making his way back to the bus station on Sunday for the return trip. One Friday the bus driver asked J.T. as he was departing the bus, "hey fella, you riding back on Sunday?" Dependent upon J.T.'s answer, the driver would never depart early on Sunday, and often wait a few extra minutes, in the event J.T. was walking because he couldn't get a ride to the bus station.

When J.T. couldn't afford bus fare he'd often hitch-hike. Over the years, he never talked of a bad experience attempting to hitch-hike to school or back home. "In those days people, would stop, black or white, and give you a ride.

"Sometimes it would take a while, most times it wouldn't. I'd keep a song in my heart to keep my spirit up." J.T. distinctly mentioned a song called, "That Lucky Old Sun." It was recorded by the great jazz musician, Louis Armstrong, in 1949. "I could listen or hum that song, and forget everything else."

"There were many times when I got on the back of a truck…sometimes 20, 30 miles, until someone made a turnoff. Then I'd get off and hitch-hike the rest of the way. Never had a bad experience."

Many years later, J.T.'s mom summed up his college travel experience in a very poignant way, which is a testament to his character and fortitude. I remember her comments almost verbatim. "He went off to college and was doing fine. Sometimes he had bus fare to come home, other times he didn't. When he didn't have money, he'd hitch-hike. He never, ever, complained. I can see him now on a Sunday, after a weekend or a holiday. He'd come to me and say, Mama, I'm getting ready to leave. Do you have a little something for me? Sometimes I would have a little piece of money for him, and sometimes I wouldn't. When I didn't have anything, he'd simply say, that's okay, Mama, I'll make it. And I couldn't look at him, but I just remember hearing the sound of that oak crutch as he made his way out of the house. It's still breaks my heart to think about it."

Chapter Twenty-One

"ROB"

J.T. beamed when he was asked to talk about his favorite instructor at Grambling. "That would have to be, Rob," he said. He was referring to none other than Grambling's legendary football coach, Eddie Robinson.

Coach Robinson had arrived on campus 7 years before J.T. in 1941. By the time J.T. arrived at Grambling, Coach Robinson had established himself as one of the best young coaches in the nation. He would go on to lead the Tiger Football team until 1997, amassing a record 408 victories, and nine black college national championships.

J.T. was enrolled in Coach Robinson's Health and Physical Education class. He remembered that "Rob always maintained full control of his class. If he was talking, you weren't." Coach Robinson took an interest in J.T. He was impressed with his attitude, and he was equally impressed with his agility and athletic ability, despite having a severe handicap.

One day, Coach engaged J.T. in a conversation regarding his college studies. J.T. didn't have a major at the time. He was completing his basic studies, and trying to decide on a career path. Coach suggested to him, "Why don't you major in education? If you do, when you graduate you're almost guaranteed to get a job teaching." J.T. heard that logic before, but coming from Coach Robinson made it resonate much more. On Coach Robinson's advice, he made the decision to major in Education. Further, he decided he would focus on Elementary Education. It would be one of the best decisions he ever made.

Chapter Twenty-Two

THE FULL
COLLEGE
EXPERIENCE

J.T. wasn't content with just attending college, he wanted to enjoy the full college experience. He became very popular on campus because of his work ethic, and his easy-going manner. He had a terrific sense of humor and could own a room and tell a good joke. People loved being in his company.

J.T. made a subtle change to his name during college. His birth name is James Thomas Martin. That name was recommended by his oldest sister, Louella (Julia), who was 10 years his senior. He never liked the name Thomas, but he did like the name, Tyrone, which happened to be the name of his favorite Hollywood movie actor at the time, Tyrone Power. So he adopted the name, Tyrone. All during his college years his friends and instructors referred to him as Tyrone.

"Tyrone" was a popular figure on campus. The college president, the legendary Ralph Waldo Emerson Jones (RWE Jones), knew him by name. President Jones was the longest serving president in the history of Grambling (1936-1977). Early in the 1950's he addressed the University during the start of a new college school year. There were many young men who were returning to school after having served a tour of duty during the Korean War. J.T. recalls a portion of President Jones' remarks, "I want to welcome back all the young men who've been away due to military service. Last semester it seemed as though the only two men left on campus was me and Tyrone." Many in the crowd burst into laughter, because they knew and liked Tyrone.

In addition to making his grades, J.T. participated in many school activities. He loved sports and although his athletic prowess was laudable, even he couldn't compete successfully in high school or college athletics while missing a leg. But that didn't stop him from being involved in athletic competition. He became an intramural softball coach. He was so engaged with the team that he would sometimes pitch at batting practice.

I personally know two members of his softball team who graduated from Grambling and who also had remarkable teaching careers in our community. They attest to his active participation on campus. They also commented favorably regarding his coaching exploits. I had to ask the question, "What was the name of your team?" I almost fell out of my chair when I heard the answer, "The Tyronians."

Chapter Twenty-Three

SEEING GREEN!

J.T. took summers off from college. During the summer he would do farm work and save money for the next semester. Something happened to him during the summer of his sophomore year that would change his life forever.

J.T. had a good friend, Sidney Davis, who he'd met out on the farm. He and Sidney hung out a lot together during the summer; they would become lifelong friends. As the story goes, one day, Sidney asked J.T. to accompany him into town. He needed to pick up some things from one of the shops and J.T. was happy to go along. As they strolled by the shops they turned off Main Street and headed south towards the dry cleaners. Sidney told J.T., "Let's stop here at the cleaners. I want to introduce you to someone."

J.T. walked in with Sidney and he can hardly remember Sidney's introduction. What he does remember, he recalled with a twinkle in his eye. "We stopped behind the counter and Sidney pointed over to his left. There I saw a fair-skinned girl hard at work. She didn't see us, just going about her business of steam pressing clothes. We watched her for a bit. She'd pull down the press on the clothes and pump the hydraulics, the steam would rise…it was something to see."

J.T. continued. "Then Sidney called out to her, Helen! She turned and I laid eyes on the prettiest girl I ever saw. She was absolutely beautiful, and very friendly," he recalled. "Her eyes were the loveliest shade of green." J.T. was smitten!

Introductions were made, and Helen Ruth Hornsby went back to work. J.T. could not contain his excitement or his interest. He wondered where she came from. Sidney explained that he'd first met Helen on the farm, and that she lived about eight miles north in a small town called, Terry. J.T. wanted to know more; Sidney explained that Helen came from a great family.

All J.T. could think of was that he wanted to get to know Helen. His next trip to the dry cleaners was without Sidney. J.T. recalls Helen being just as nice the second time he saw her. He told her about his family, that he was a college man at home for the summer, and he'd like to get to know her better.

Alas the summer was over, and it was time to get back to school. J.T. made a commitment to Helen. He told her, after just a few months, that he wanted to marry her. Helen liked J.T. but she was not yet convinced they were right for each other. She kept the door open.

Years later, J.T. would tell a story to his children that Helen happily confirmed. "When I got back to college for that Fall

Semester after meeting your mom, I wrote her a letter every single day! I mean every day; do you hear me?" Helen happily confirmed J.T.'s act of love. "Yes, he did. He wrote me the sweetest letters. I received one almost every day for three months when we were courting. They got lost somehow. I wish to God I had kept them."

Chapter Twenty-Four

Philippians 4:13

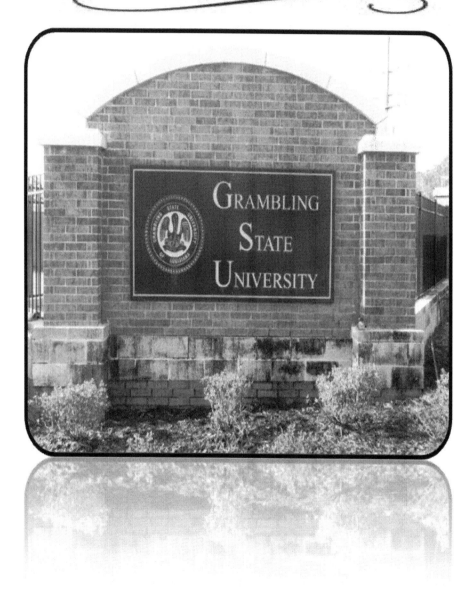

As a full-fledged college senior, in the fall of 1952, J.T.'s classroom work took on an entirely different meaning. He was now ready for Student Teaching, a requirement for Elementary Education majors who were preparing to enter the teaching profession. He completed his initial iteration on campus at Grambling High School. In the spring semester of 1953, he completed his final phase of Student Teaching at Morehouse Parish, located in the town of Bastrop, Louisiana.

The final phase of student teaching was very rewarding in many respects. Number one, he received a monthly stipend to help defray the travel expenses. Number two, at the end of this phase he'd have all the course work and hours required to graduate. Number three, and most important to J.T. at the time, was that the Bastrop assignment was only 35 miles from home. This allowed him to complete his college requirements, while being close to Helen, who had agreed to marry him after he finished college.

In the summer of 1953, J.T. completed what was considered by most of his contemporaries to be an impossible journey-a little boy who cheated death, started school at age nine, grew up dirt poor during the Great Depression--in the home of a sharecropper-would walk across the stage at Grambling College and receive his Bachelor of Arts Degree in Elementary Education.

J.T. made the decision to walk across the stage using his one crutch, and not the bulky prosthesis, which he utilized in the classroom during his student teaching (so as not to distract the young children). He had never been ashamed of his handicap; he never used it as an excuse. His Grambling College family had observed and admired his grit and determination for nearly five years, as he traversed to classes and school events, up and down the hills of Grambling College, using one crutch. They would see it once more as he made his way down the graduation line and up on the stage to receive his diploma.

His classmates and members of the faculty and staff at Grambling roared when his name was called, "James TYRONE Martin." No surprises from his mom, siblings, or Helen, who was also in attendance. He'd informed them all months prior to, that he had adopted the middle name, Tyrone.

What a proud day for his mom. She recalled the event many times over the years. "Sometimes I wondered if he'd make it. But he stuck with it. I've never seen him give up on anything.

It was a proud day for us. I met many of J.T.'s teachers and friends. They were all very nice. I just thanked the Lord."

Chapter Twenty-Five

VAULTING OVER DESTINY...

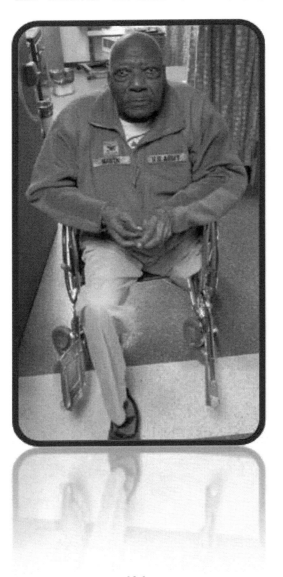

At the age of 24, J.T. had a lot to be proud of. Against all odds, he had become the first male in his family to earn a college degree. He accepted a teaching position at an elementary school not far from where he attended high school. And most importantly, he got the girl!

J.T. and Helen embarked upon a life journey which has now spanned seven decades. They reared eleven children who are all high school graduates and who are all firmly rooted in the Christian faith.

There have been many peaks and a few valleys over the years. But God's grace and mercy have been bountiful on their family over their 63-plus years of marriage.

Growing up the way he did during the Great Depression, as the son of a dirt-poor sharecropper in the Jim Crow south, J.T.'s prospects for raising his standard of living were dim. He was destined to be a ward of the state, or someone who scratched out a living doing farm work or unskilled labor.

But from the start, J.T. was exceptional. He challenged himself to achieve and he never entertained self-pity. As a young boy, he learned to utilize his crutch to propel himself over fences.

In the same manner, he literally propelled himself to success, and exceeded all the average expectations many had for his life.

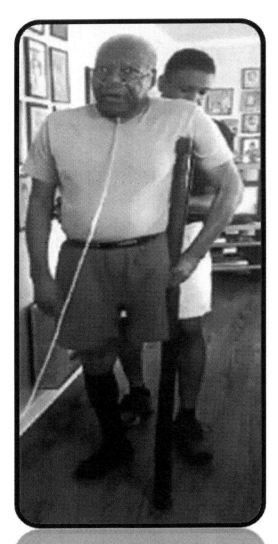

His destiny was not sealed on the morning of his horrific accident, or by the lot of his birth. With God's help, he vaulted over it all. Throughout his life, those who have come to know him have not referred to him as a handicapped man….but simply, a man!

It all started with a strong-willed little boy who refused to go quietly after a devastating injury. The ministry of angels released on that tragic morning, have followed him and favored him for nearly 90 years.

EPILOGUE

The story of James Tyrone Martin, Sr., my dad, is an exciting and colorful one. In this body of work, I decided to focus on his very humble beginnings. If there was ever someone who personified the phrase, "pulled himself up by his bootstraps," he is among that rarified air. Expectations for a severely handicapped black child growing up the son of a sharecropper in that type of daunting environment were demonstrably low.

In the same way that he overcame his physical challenges-learning to use his one crutch to vault himself over a fence-he symbolically vaulted over his destiny. He was destined to be a ward of the state or the federal government. As a sharecropper's son, he was destined for a life in a similar vein but he wanted more. He continued to meet every challenge, exceed every expectation.

His quest for ordinary treatment and access was matched by his desire to meet any physical challenge that treatment required. In achieving that quest, he became extraordinary, vaulting over his destiny; the lot in life dictated by his birthright.

After college, J.T. became an elementary school teacher at Magnolia School in Pioneer, Louisiana. He enjoyed a very successful teaching career, which spanned 30 years. During his tenure, he positively influenced thousands of young children, who later became highly successful professionals, serving today in communities across the state and throughout the nation. Dad spoke highly about the professional relationship and friendship he enjoyed with two great educators while at Magnolia; school principals Grady Murphy, and the late Quitman Durbin.

At his best, I would offer that he is the kind of guy you'd love to have a root beer soda with. He is a magnificent storyteller, has a terrific sense of humor, and a really great comedic timing. Anyone in the community will tell you that Dad is a master at telling a joke. But don't get too close because he tends to slap you on the leg when he delivers a punch line.

Dad loves a good movie, although he feels, "Hollywood don't make 'em like they used to." In their prime, he really enjoyed Sidney Poitier, Gregory Peck, Spencer Tracy, and Bing Crosby. Today, Denzel Washington is at the top of his list of favorite actors who embraced the screen. Among his favorite movies are "In the Heat of the Night," "To Kill a Mockingbird," "White Christmas," and "Guess Who's Coming to Dinner."

Through the years, we became familiar with his favorite recording artists. He has a terrific voice and while working or shaving, he always hummed and sung a few bars from hits by his favorite artists like Nat King Cole, Frank Sinatra, Ray Charles, Louis Armstrong, and Roy Rogers and Dale Evans.

Dad absolutely loves Gospel music. The great Mahalia Jackson is at the top of his list. "Precious Lord" and "His Eye is on the Sparrow" are two standards that Dad often hummed around the house when we were growing up. I asked him what his all-time favorite recording was and he replied, "I can't really say for sure, but one tune that's been on my mind a bit lately is 'Looking Back Over My Life,' by Nat King Cole. Boy, I tell ya, now that's a song!" In addition to Mr. Cole's absolutely pure vocals, perhaps it's the reflective lyrics which stir the soul of my nearly 89 year old dad, a true "Lion in Winter."

Dad loves sports-boxing, football, basketball, and baseball. Joe Louis, Sugar Ray Robinson, and Muhammad Ali, were his favorite boxers. He'll tell you today that "pound for pound Sugar Ray Robinson might have been the best." He believes that the legendary NFL Hall of Famer, Jim Brown, is the best football player ever, and if you ask him who was the best on the baseball diamond he'll give you a long answer. "I loved to see Hank Aaron, Jackie Robinson, and ole Mickey Mantle. They were all great. But the best overall was Willie Mays."

His favorite all-time NBA basketball team was the 1970 World Champion New York Knicks, led by their captain and NBA Hall of Famer, Willis Reed, a former Grambling College standout. Dad's baby brother, 6'7" Kenneth Martin, played alongside Reed at Grambling College in the early sixties. After his sophomore year, Uncle Kenneth's promising career and life was cut short, as he was diagnosed with cancer and transitioned shortly thereafter in 1964. (Please see his 1963 basketball yearbook photo on page 84).

Dad's love of farming never left his system. He raised a large garden of vegetables every year. Even into his fifties, when his sons were teenagers, he set the pace for planting, harvesting, and keeping the rows clean. At that point, we no longer marveled at his ability, despite his handicap. We just thought that's just Dad being Dad.

Dad is frugal but perhaps that's somewhat common for a depression era child. He doesn't like to waste food or money, his 30-40-year-old sport coats are still in fine condition, and he always keeps his cars for 10-15 years.

For the past 10-15 years, before suffering a severe illness, might have been among his best. He served with absolute distinction on the West Carroll Parish School Board, becoming the first African American elected to serve on the board. He won re-election three times, served on the board for nearly two decades, including a tenure as the school board president.

He speaks with immense pride regarding his professional and personal relationships with four "outstanding school board superintendents: Jerry Dosher, Roger Kent Davis, Richard Strong, and Donald K. Gwin."

While serving as school board president, he often traveled across the State of Louisiana attending educational conferences and seminars. He loved being accompanied by his lovely wife during those awesome trips.

He served with humility and honor at Church Street Church of God, as a Sunday school superintendent, becoming the first African American elected to serve on the Board. He was never late, often opened the Church, and diligently prepared himself to teach Sunday school or during Wednesday night prayer meetings. He was a rock of stability in the Church, under the pastoral tutelage of his son, Joseph.

Dad loves West Carroll Parish and Oak Grove, Louisiana. And they love him back, and respect him for the inspirational manner in which he has lived his life, despite overwhelming adversity.

He and his lovely Helen have been married for over 63 years. My siblings and I have always thought that Mom was the perfect complement to Dad. She was a rock of stability, fiercely loyal, and a consistent well-spring of love. Mom worked for the State of Louisiana for over two decades, winning the prestigious Charles E. Dunbar, Jr. Civil Service Award in 1991, as the "Older Worker of the Year." In the early 1990's, she was one of

Louisiana's early recipients of former President George H.W. Bush's, Thousand Points of Light Award for outstanding volunteer contributions to her community in Oak Grove, Louisiana.

It has been my distinct pleasure and a labor of love to work on this project, which includes all the stories at family gatherings, shared by uncles and aunts, and my grandma, Lucy. I was blessed to have countless conversations over the years with Dad regarding his early life. Many of those conversations carried over into the wee hours of the morning. The first-hand account of Mr. Shorty McDaniel, a longtime family friend, who was the first on the scene to get to Dad immediately after his accident at the sawmill. It was emotionally taxing to write about, but quite necessary, for its significant and compelling testament to Dad's outstanding resiliency.

Dad (and Mom for that matter) is a solid member of the "Greatest Generation of Americans," the World War II generation coined by the great journalist and broadcaster, Tom Brokaw, in his 1998 book of the same name. He faced hardships with a fighting spirit, and an indomitable will. Never complained, never saw his achievements or overcoming his lot in life as heroic.

The year 2014 was a year of transition for Dad and Mom. After collapsing and nearly dying, he was diagnosed with an advanced case of Chronic Obstructive Pulmonary Disease. He'd been symptomatic for several years, but true to his nature of never complaining, he soldiered on. Dad was truly blessed to be able to remain home for a couple of years after the attack, largely due to around the clock care provided by Mom, my sisters, Marcia and Mona, and the significant contributions of my brother, Joseph, sister Pauline, and sister-in-law, Ruthie.

After another setback, early in 2016, due to the deteriorating nature of his illness, he had to transition to a care facility. After 63 years, Mom and Dad would be physically separated at night. It was an emotionally draining experience for our entire family.

The outstanding care facility, West Carroll Parish Health Systems where he now resides, is only a mile from Mom and Dad's house. The facility is outstanding. It's very well operated and the care providers are a Godsend. At 91 years young, Mom is still driving and she makes the trek nearly every day to spend time with him.

On September 19, 2017, Dad will celebrate his 89th birthday. He's doing well. Takes therapy three or four days a week, and enjoys reading, studying the Bible, watching sports, and winning money playing dominoes and bingo with friends.

Dad's miracle filled life, coupled with he and Mom's blessed union, are a testament to the Lord Jesus' boundless grace and unconditional love. I feel blessed to have had the honor and the privilege of capturing and preserving a remarkable portion of Dad's history for our family, and for generations of others as well. Thank God for the little boy who cheated death, and lived to comb gray hair.

ACKNOWLEDGEMENTS

The Martin Family
**Left-right front: Helen and James Martin, Sr.
Second row: Mona, Josephine, Pauline, and Marcia.
Back row: Red, Joseph, J.T. Jr., Eddie, Nathan,
Jeremy M. and Kenneth**

I am grateful to my beautiful and talented wife, Ava, for her patience, and editing skills, as she worked diligently to keep me focused during this project. I can always count on Ava to render a "candid" opinion. Her abiding love and loyalty are the fuel that powers our family.

It was tremendously helpful to bounce ideas off my son, Nick, during this process; one Dad writing about another Dad, and discussing relevant and sometimes sensitive thoughts with his son.

My daughter, Rachel, an aspiring writer in her second year of college, was also quite helpful. Rachel is a voracious reader, and her observations were helpful beyond measure.

To Mom and Dad, it's my high honor and great privilege to be your son. I thank God I was born into such a wonderful, loving, and God fearing family.

I salute my older brothers and sisters, from the eldest to the youngest: Nathan, Pauline, Eddie, Joseph, Josephine, J.T. Jr., Marcia, and Mona. I want to thank you from the bottom of my heart for your love, and your wise counsel to me and my children. I am honored and privileged to be your little brother.

For my two younger brothers, Kenneth and Red, I love you as well. From this day forward, I promise I will continue to work hard to be the loving big brother to you that my older siblings have been to me.

To Aunt Mable; thank you for your love and encouragement, and for sharing so many wonderful stories of your childhood growing up with Dad.

To Mr. Shorty McDaniel, a family friend who passed away nearly 2 decades ago, we thank God for you, Mr. Shorty -- that you were the first on the scene to help Dad on that fateful morning in 1930.

To Trish Geran for her unwavering commitment and outstanding professionalism in guiding us through this book project. I've never worked with a more skillful or stellar professional. My family and I are eternally grateful to you for your diligence and your patience.

To Roosevelt Toston; trailblazer, mentor, and family friend. Thank you for your friendship, and your sterling example which served as a catalyst for this book project.

To Candance Williams, for your spirited encouragement and enthusiasm during the writing of this book.

To Dr. Charles and Mrs. Joy Bole; I hereby proclaim you, "Honorary Louisianans!" Thanks for your encouragement and unwavering support!

To Dr. Michael Oldham, thanks for your steadfast support, and the azimuth check.

To every teacher who taught me over the years. Thank you for investing in me. Of particular note, my first and fourth grade teachers from Combs McIntyre High School, Mrs. Embra McDade and Mrs. Mattie Cockerham. You ladies are simply the best. My outstanding Sunday school teacher, Mrs. Edna Toston, who has gone on to Glory, but is frequently in my thoughts. Professor Eddie Jones, my English and speech professor from Grambling State University. He taught us English, he taught us about life, and he really cared. And finally, to Dr. Jim Gordon and Dr. Craig Nation, my professors at the United States Army War College. I learned a great deal about Strategic Planning in their Seminar 19 classroom (Flagship Seminar), and I learned a great deal about myself, after a year under their professional tutelage.

I acknowledge and thank the Honorable Les Brownlee, former Acting Secretary of the Army, for his encouragement concerning this project. It was fifteen years ago, while accompanying him as his Media Spokesperson, that he strongly suggested I compile a history of my dad's life. He believed Dad's history to be a great American story of perseverance and courage. I agree with my old boss.

And finally, to Uncle Poodah, who transitioned to heaven earlier this year, just month's shy of his 98th birthday. Thanks for looking out for Dad and Aunt Mable during those early years and for your love and kindness.

Just the mention of Uncle Poodah always brought a big smile to Dad's face. Their relationship was strong, and he said they never had a cross word. They were similar in so many ways.

Both very stoic, rarely complained about anything, and were grateful for the life they lived and the times they shared. They were two brothers who laughed heartily about growing up during the Great Depression. "We could look up at the ceiling at night and see the stars, or look through the floor and see the chickens."

As Uncle Poodah cruised into his nineties, he was still up and about every morning, walking a mile or so around his neighborhood, and preparing breakfast for Aunt Lela, his lovely wife of 74 years. On many occasions, I heard my dad report with pride, "I talked with ole Poodah today. That son of a gun walked a mile this morning…walks it every day!"

Dad and Uncle Poodah used to try and visit each other annually; Dad would make a family trip to Texas City, Texas, where Poodah lived, or Poodah would return home to Oak Grove. Over the past several years, the brothers were unable to travel or visit each other due to health complications, so instead they spoke frequently by phone.

Nothing is more indicative of the bond they shared than the dream Dad experienced, as Uncle Poodah was passing away into eternity earlier this year. When my sister, Marcia, informed him that his big brother had transitioned, Dad paused, and a warm smile enveloped his face. "I just had a dream about Poodah! In my dream, we were out on a golf course playing golf together. We were having a good time, ole Poodah was laughing and we were having a lot of fun." Now truth be told, Dad nor Uncle Poodah to my knowledge, ever played a round of golf. Why did God allow Dad to experience such a wonderful dream?

I believe God extended His awesome grace to the brothers, by allowing Dad to see Poodah once again, at peace, in health, and in awesome fellowship with the little brother he loved so much. Given their humble beginnings on the farm, where preparing the land was a way of life, they must have so enjoyed the lush fairways and manicured greens on the heavenly golf course God allowed Dad to experience with his brother. With nary a tear and no regrets, Dad said, "Ole Poodah lived a great life. I know I'll see him again and we'll have a good ole time."

ABOUT THE AUTHOR

Jeremy M. Martin is number nine of eleven children born to James T. Sr. and Helen Martin. He grew up in northeast Louisiana, a rural farming community in the town of Oak Grove. He is a graduate of Oak Grove High School, and Grambling State University, where he earned a bachelor's degree in political science.

While at Grambling, he enrolled in the Army ROTC program. He was selected as a distinguished ROTC graduate, and commissioned a Second Lieutenant in the United States Army. Colonel Martin served with distinction in the Infantry, Military Intelligence Corps, and as a highly decorated Public Affairs Officer over the final 13 years of his active duty Army career.

Over the course of his career, Colonel Martin earned a master's degree from Webster University (Human Resources Development) and the United States Army War College (Strategic Studies). He has also completed graduate work with the University of Oklahoma, and Liberty University.

In 2011, he became the first African American to be selected to command the prestigious Defense Information School, the Department of Defense's premier school for Public Affairs and Visual Information training.

After 30 years of honorable and distinguished service, he retired in 2015 at the rank of Colonel. In the summer of 2016, he was elected into the inaugural class of the National Army ROTC

Hall of Fame, along with such luminaries as: General (Ret.) Colin L. Powell; current Supreme Court Justice, Samuel Alito; and legendary National Football League Hall of Famer, Jim Brown.

In 2015, he accepted an appointment to serve in the administration of the first African American president in the history of the United States, Barack Obama. Colonel Martin served as a Senior Executive on the staff of the Secretary of Defense, as the Chief of Staff for the Assistant Secretary of Defense, and Pentagon Press Secretary, while concurrently performing the duties as the Deputy Assistant Secretary of Defense for Community and Public Outreach, and the Principal Deputy Assistant Secretary of Defense for Public Affairs, the second highest ranking Public Affairs position in the Department of Defense.

Colonel Martin has received numerous awards and decorations during his distinguished career which included: the Military Outstanding Volunteer Service Medal; the Meritorious and Joint Meritorious Service Medals; the Legion of Merit; the Defense Superior Service Medal; and in January of 2017, he was awarded the Secretary of Defense Medal for Outstanding Civilian Service.

Colonel Martin enjoys spending time with his lovely wife, Ava, and family. He enjoys Christian outreach, reading, exercising, and volunteering in the community.

Made in the USA
Columbia, SC
13 October 2017